Facts About the Tapir

By Lisa Strattin

© 2020 Lisa Strattin

FREE BOOK

FOR ALL SUBSCRIBERS SIGN UP NOW FOR MY SPAM FREE NEWSLETTER

LisaStrattin.com/Subscribe-Here

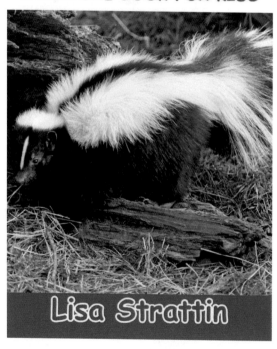

FACTS ABOUT THE
SKUNK
A PICTURE BOOK FOR KIDS

Lisa Strattin

Facts for Kids Picture Books by Lisa Strattin

Little Blue Penguin, Vol 92

Chipmunk, Vol 5

Frilled Lizard, Vol 39

Blue and Gold Macaw, Vol 13

Poison Dart Frogs, Vol 50

Blue Tarantula, Vol 115

African Elephants, Vol 8

Amur Leopard, Vol 89

Sabre Tooth Tiger, Vol 167

Baboon, Vol 174

Sign Up for New Release Emails Here

http://LisaStrattin.com/subscribe-here

COVER IMAGE

https://www.flickr.com/photos/7326810@N08/1072909038/

ADDITIONAL IMAGES

https://www.flickr.com/photos/12587661@N06/11654780264/

https://www.flickr.com/photos/vonguard/3554786437/

https://www.flickr.com/photos/schmeeve/309170282/

https://www.flickr.com/photos/15016964@N02/5512293925/

https://www.flickr.com/photos/phalinn/4256375923/

https://www.flickr.com/photos/15016964@N02/4505466839/

https://www.flickr.com/photos/ekilby/29840623982/

https://www.flickr.com/photos/dalangalma/65276833/

https://www.flickr.com/photos/zooeurope/20848673108/

https://www.flickr.com/photos/ekilby/16839260592/

Contents

INTRODUCTION

The Tapir looks like a pig, but is a large mammal that is believed to be more closely related to Rhinos and Horses.

SPECIES

Tapirs have been identified as four different species:

- The Baird's Tapir is native to Central America and has cream colored marking on their face.

- The Malayan Tapir (sometimes called the Asian Tapir) is the largest of the four species. They have a white band all across their body.

- The Mountain Tapir lives in the high Andes Mountain forests of Columbia, Peru and Ecuador. They are the smallest of the four different species.

- The Brazilian Tapir (sometimes called the South American Tapir) is a very good swimmer and usually lives close to water in the region of the Amazon Rainforest.

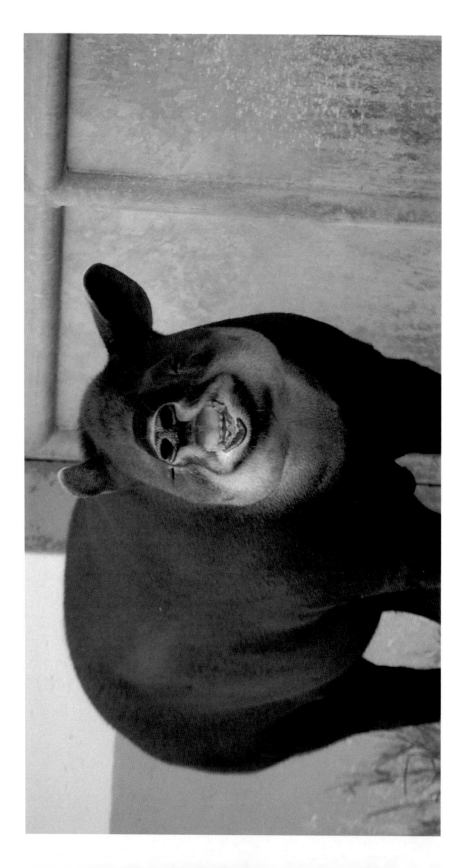

APPEARANCE

All Tapirs have a very long, flexible nose – like a smaller version of an Elephant's trunk. They use their nose to grab branches that hang low in the forest and to get the lush plants out of the waterways near where they live. They all swim, even though the Brazilian Tapir is known to be the best swimmer.

They will not hesitate to go into the water to get a plant to eat. They seem to be as comfortable in water as a Rhinoceros.

They can be white, black, gray or brown.

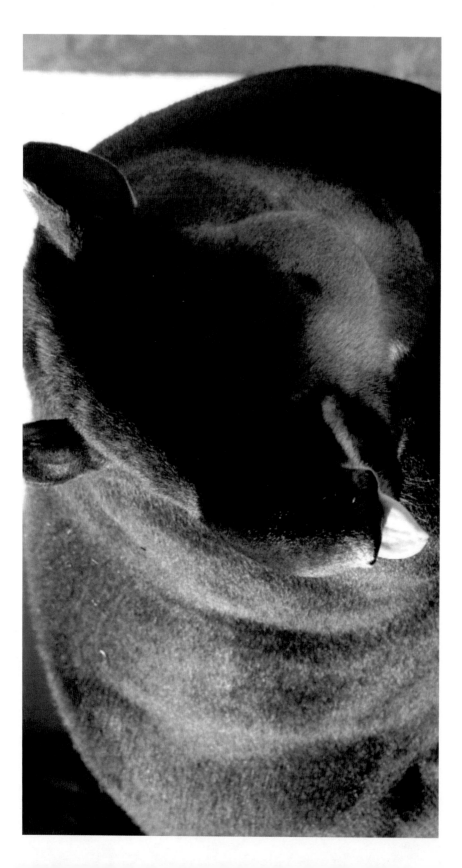

REPRODUCTION

The Tapir usually mates in April and May because these are cooler months where they live. The female is pregnant for a full year with one baby!

The baby Tapir is born with stripes on their coat, instead of the colors that you normally see on adults. The baby leaves the mother to live on its own when it becomes two to three years old.

LIFE SPAN

Tapirs can live to be 25 years old.

SIZE

Adult Tapirs weigh between 300 and 700 pounds! They grow to be three to six feet long. They are very big, so you can see why scientists believe they are related to the Rhinoceros!

HABITAT

Tapirs live in the temperate, wet areas of the Southern Hemisphere. They are found in many countries of South America.

DIET

Tapirs eat plants. They like branches, twigs, shoots, fruits, berries and the plants that grow in the water. They spend a lot of time foraging for food.

ENEMIES

The Tapir is very big, so there are not a lot of natural predators that it has to worry about. But the wild cats: Jaguars, Lions, Cougars will hunt and kill them for food. Also, Crocodiles will kill them in the water if they get the chance. Now and then, a large snake has been known to kill and eat a Tapir, but not as often as the big wild cats.

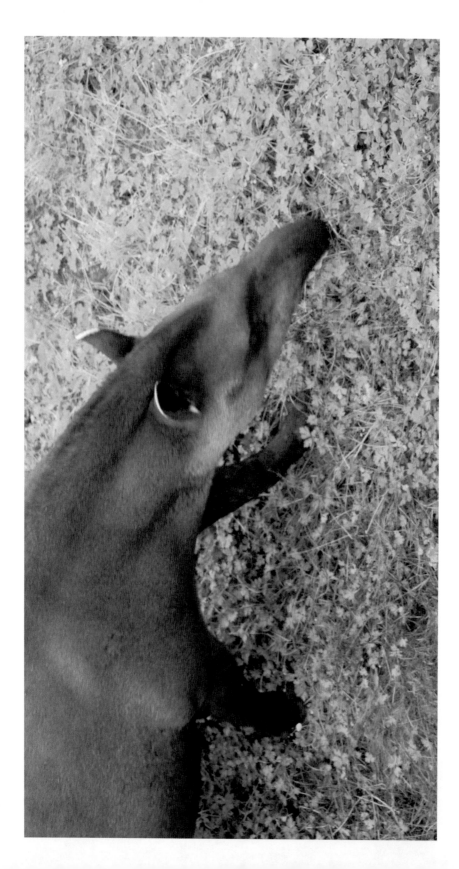

SUITABILITY AS PETS

Some people have kept Tapirs as pets. But they are not for everyone. You need to have a large area for them, because they need to be able to roam around looking for plants to eat, both on land and in the water.

In some areas, it is not legal to keep a Tapir, so you definitely should check the local laws where you live to make sure that you won't get in trouble.

They are very big too. You would also need to make sure that your veterinarian knows enough about the pet you choose in order to treat it appropriately when it needs medical attention.

Even if it is legal where you live, you might want a smaller animal like a dog or cat that is easier to care for.

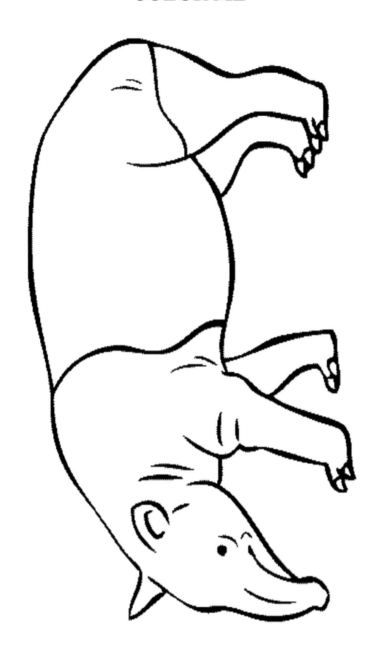

COLOR ME

COLOR ME

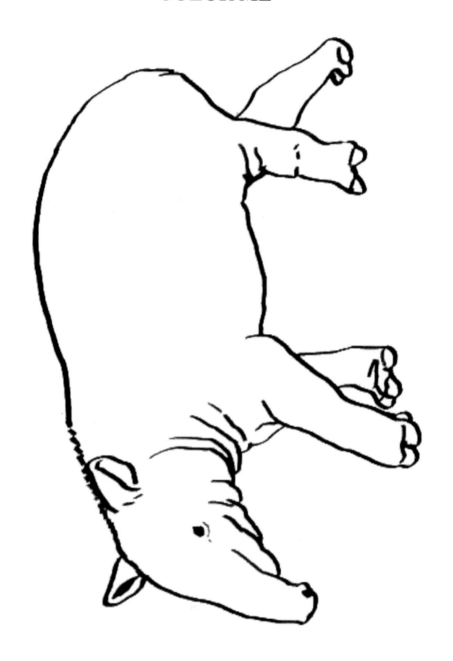

COLOR ME

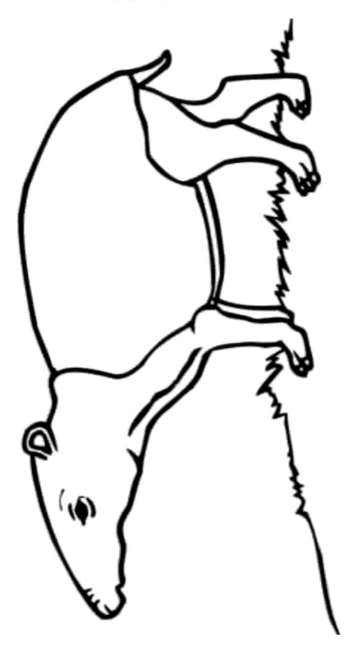

COLOR ME

COLOR ME

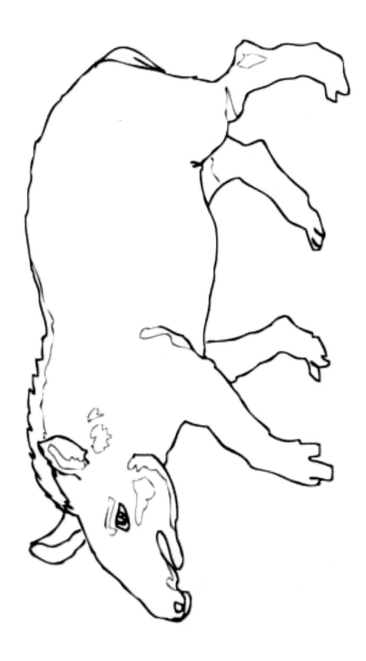

Please leave me a review here:

http://lisastrattin.com/Review-Vol-364

For more Kindle Downloads Visit Lisa Strattin Author Page on Amazon Author Central

http://amazon.com/author/lisastrattin

To see upcoming titles, visit my website at LisaStrattin.com– all books available on kindle!

http://lisastrattin.com

FREE BOOK

FOR ALL SUBSCRIBERS – SIGN UP NOW

FOR MY SPAM-FREE NEWSLETTER

LisaStrattin.com/Subscribe-Here

Made in the USA
Columbia, SC
02 December 2020